fresh
in autumn

fresh
in autumn

cooking with Alastair Hendy
photography by David Loftus

Macmillan Canada
Toronto

First published in Canada in 2000
by Macmillan Canada,
an imprint of CDG Books Canada

Text © Alastair Hendy 1999
Design and photographs
© Ryland Peters & Small 1999

Printed and bound in China by Toppan Printing Co.

Canadian Cataloguing in Publication Data

Hendy, Alastair
  Fresh in autumn

Includes index.
ISBN 0-7715-7661-7

1. Cookery. 2. Autumn. I. Title.

TX714.H4622 2000   641.5'64   C99-932430-6

Special sales

This book is available at special discounts for bulk
purchases by your group or organization for sales
promotions, premiums, fundraising and seminars. For
details, contact: CDG Books Canada Inc., 99 Yorkville
Avenue, Suite 400, Toronto, ON, M5R 3K5

Notes
Cooking and eating wrongly identified mushrooms can
be fatal. If in doubt, don't. Neither the author nor the
publishers can ever accept any legal responsibility or
liability for any errors, omissions, or mistaken
identification of fungus species that may be made.
All spoon measurements are level unless otherwise noted.
Specialty Asian ingredients are available in large
supermarkets, Thai, Chinese, Japanese, and
Vietnamese shops, as well as Asian stores.
Raw or partly cooked eggs should not be served to the
very young, the old, the frail, or to pregnant women.

1 2 3 4 5 RPS 04 03 02 01 00

Dedication

To my mother

contents

introduction   7

squash   8

nuts   24

mushrooms   38

apples   52

pears   66

index   80

To me, Autumn means the fruits of the field, orchard, and forest; pumpkins of all shapes and hides; fresh nuts; a complete compendium of mushrooms; bags of apples and pears. It means slow-cooked stews with layers of flavor; braises, bakes, and roasts, and a full quota of comforting desserts. This book is for everyone —cooks and non-cooks, for those who are just starting, and for those who like others to cook for them. If you're not an accomplished cook or haven't had much practice, just follow the recipe and all should be well. It's how I learned to cook—from books. My mother spent time in the kitchen cooking for the family but wasn't always too keen on engaging eager-to-help little hands. If I offered to cook supper she'd happily stay clear— offering advice from afar (her bath). I was forever being told to look it up in "the book" (but which book she meant, I was never quite sure). So I now know how important it is for a recipe to be accurate, so that it works and tastes good. My mother's brand of "tuition" was spot-on.

Fresh in Autumn has short, quick recipes to give you instant satisfaction— and others that will need time in the oven and, for some, a well-earned snooze on the sofa. It's for everyone who loves food. And for those who dream of a picture-perfect season of so-called mellow fruitfulness, the gentle warmth of the oven with its promise of dinner, steamy windows, and pot-roast aromas. Perfect.

7

Squash don't look real. They don't look like food either. Outrageously shaped, knobbled and gnarled, they look positively extra-terrestrial. Some, like acorn squash, look like grenades, butternut squash defy description, whereas the big jolly orange ones are most at home when etched with a big toothy cartoon grin—with names like Hubbard, Turk's Cap, and Munchkins. With hides like old leather, they are the true eccentrics of the vegetable patch.

Inside they are tender and sweet. The flesh is dense yet delicate when cooked; bold in flavor and color—yet sensuous and light. Don't just relegate them to a decorative role—they are the edible stars of Fall.

Pumpkins, butternut squash, zucchini, Chinese winter melons, pattypan squash, and other squash (of which their are hundreds of varieties) all belong to the *Cucurbita* genus of edible gourds. In this book, I've used the varieties that are at their best in Fall. Zucchini and other squashes with edible skins belong to the summer kitchen. Butternut and acorn squash both have excellent flavor and so do the large, lobed varieties with leathery skins—these can usually be bought in more manageable cut pieces.

Pumpkins can be baked whole in their skins, roasted in sections, boiled, or steamed. Don't be afraid to experiment—pumpkin can handle it. Apart from making soup (one of my favorites—particularly good with sautéed apple and salty cheese stirred in), and classic American pumpkin pie, you can add it to casseroles, braises, and tagines. It's brilliant with spices, or doused with olive oil, flavored with herbs and roasted alongside onions; thick slices can be baked with butter, then topped with cheese and broiled; steamed nuggets can be stirred into creamy risotto and pasta.

So if you're still one of the unconverted, next time you spot a squash, add him to your shopping basket and experiment—you'll discover beauty's much more than (knobbly) skin deep.

squash

Pumpkin soup

with Creole roasted pumpkin seeds and goat cheese

A bowl of hot pumpkin soup on a cold wet fall day—just add a slice or three of goat cheese and a good sprinkling of crisp pumpkin seeds and your soup will turn into a meal. Use dense-fleshed pumpkin with brown, gray, or dark green skins—orange-skinned varieties tend to be watery.

3 lb. pumpkin, halved and peeled

olive oil, for sautéing and baking

1 onion, finely chopped

2 garlic cloves, crushed

2 teaspoons cumin seeds, toasted

2 sprigs of thyme

2 bay leaves

½ teaspoon freshly grated nutmeg

1 teaspoon ground allspice

1½ quarts chicken stock

salt and freshly ground black pepper

1 ash-crust goat cheese log
or 1 small tub of goat curd cheese,
to serve

Creole roasted pumpkin seeds:

2 teaspoons olive oil

½ teaspoon garlic salt

½ teaspoon onion powder

1 teaspoon paprika

a pinch of cayenne

1 teaspoon dried oregano

Serves 4

1

Remove and reserve the pumpkin seeds. Cut the pumpkin flesh into large chunks.

2

Heat 2 tablespoons olive oil in a deep skillet, add the onion and garlic, and sauté until soft. Add salt and pepper, the cumin seeds, thyme, bay leaves, nutmeg, and allspice. Sauté for 1 minute. Add the stock and pumpkin and simmer gently for about 30 minutes or until soft. Purée in a food processor, transfer to a saucepan, and keep it warm.

3

Clean the fibers off the pumpkin seeds, then toss the seeds with the olive oil, garlic salt, onion powder, paprika, cayenne, and oregano. Spread over a baking tray and roast in a preheated oven at 400°F for 10–15 minutes.

4

Serve the soup accompanied by the toasted seeds and slices of goat cheese.

Variations:
• Replace the toasted pumpkin seeds with fried crispy sage leaves.
• Use freshly grated Parmesan or Gruyère instead of goat cheese.

Pumpkin fondue with artichokes and sage

A hybrid dish—a mixture of Swiss fondue, pumpkin soup, plus classic artichoke and cheese dip. And it's sublime. The baked pumpkin and runny cheese flavored with sage and artichokes are magic together. Dip in with breadsticks and scoop out the pumpkin with spoons (make sure your friends are well acquainted with each other—this is communal dining).

1 medium flat pumpkin

½ teaspoon freshly grated nutmeg

¼ cup butter

1 onion, very finely chopped

1 garlic clove, crushed

⅔ cup dry white wine

1 teaspoon all-purpose flour

5 sprigs of sage, chopped

2 teaspoons dried oregano

4 baby artichokes in oil, drained and chopped

1¼ lb. Emmental or Gruyère cheese (or a mixture), grated

½ cup sour cream

salt and freshly ground black pepper

green Tabasco, to taste (optional)

Caraway grissini:

1 lb. package bread mix or ciabatta mix

1 tablespoon dried oregano

1 tablespoon caraway seeds

olive oil, for greasing

melted butter, for brushing

semolina flour, for dusting

Serves 4

1

To make the grissini, follow the package instructions to the first rising of the dough, then divide in half. Add the oregano to one half and the caraway seeds to the other, and knead again. Roll out each piece to ⅛ inch thick and slice into 1-inch wide strips. Put, spaced apart, on a baking tray greased with olive oil and let rise in a warm place for 10 minutes. Brush with melted butter, dust with semolina flour, and bake in a preheated oven at 450°F for 15 minutes or until golden brown.

2

Slice the top off the pumpkin and reserve it, hollow out the core, and discard all the fibers and seeds. Rub with salt, pepper, and nutmeg, and smear the inside with half the butter. Put into a roasting pan and bake in a preheated oven at 350°F for 45 minutes to 1 hour, or until almost cooked.

3

Heat the remaining butter in a skillet, add the onion and garlic, and sauté until soft and translucent. Add the wine, heat to simmering, then add all the remaining ingredients, except the sour cream, and stir until the cheese melts.

4

Spoon the cheese mixture into the pumpkin, stir in the sour cream, replace the lid, and continue baking for about 20 minutes. Serve with grissini and spoons.

Acorn squash with ginger and seaweed

Acorn squash has dense golden flesh. It's a little difficult to peel as it is so deeply ribbed—cutting it up first then peeling the wedges is the best way to tackle it. It suits these Japanese flavors and is especially good with grated fresh ginger. Add noodles and you have a complete meal.

3 bundles Asian noodles, such as ramen or udon (optional)

1 oz. dried hijiki or wakame seaweed*

1 small acorn squash, about 1½ lb.

2 cups dashi (use instant dashi and follow the package instructions)*

3 tablespoons mirin (sweetened rice wine)*

1 tablespoon sugar

¼ cup light soy sauce

1 inch fresh ginger, finely sliced and shredded, to serve

Serves 4

*Note: *Seaweed, dashi, and mirin are sold in Asian markets, and often available in larger supermarkets.*

1

Cook the noodles, if using, for about 2 minutes in boiling water until *al dente*. Rinse in cold water, drain, then let return to room temperature.

2

Put the seaweed into a bowl of cold water until soft and rehydrated. Drain.

3

Cut the squash into quarters, deseed, peel, slice each piece in half crosswise, then again lengthwise.

4

Put the squash into a saucepan, add the dashi, mirin, sugar, and soy sauce, bring to a boil, then simmer for 15 minutes. Add the drained seaweed and warm through for 1 minute.

5

Divide the noodles between 4 bowls, add the squash, seaweed, and a ladle of hot stock. Top with shredded ginger, or serve separately, so people can help themselves.

Variations:

• Instead of seaweed add finely shredded scallion or stems of watercress.

Pumpkin coconut curry

Make this curry with ordinary pumpkin, or with spaghetti squash—melon-shaped, with yellow flesh that pulls into strands when cooked. I prefer to bake it first before adding to the curry, to retain the long strands.

1 lb. spaghetti squash or pumpkin, peeled, seeded, and cut into chunks

10 small shallots, finely sliced lengthwise

4 garlic cloves, crushed

½ teaspoon turmeric

1 inch fresh ginger, chopped

2 stalks lemongrass, finely chopped

1 tablespoon red Thai curry paste

3 tablespoons salted cashews

4 tablespoons peanut oil, plus extra for brushing

1 teaspoon tamarind paste
or 1 tablespoon fresh lemon juice

1¾ cups canned coconut milk

¾ cup chicken or vegetable stock

salt

To serve:

fresh cilantro leaves

fresh beansprouts

Serves 4

1

If using spaghetti squash, brush it with a little oil and salt, then bake in a preheated oven at 375°F for 30–45 minutes until cooked. Pull the flesh into strings. If using regular pumpkin, cut it into bite-sized chunks.

2

Place 4 shallots, the garlic, turmeric, ginger, lemongrass, Thai curry paste, and cashews into an electric blender and process to a coarse paste.

3

Heat 2 tablespoons of the oil in a skillet, add the paste, and sauté until it darkens in color, adding a drop more oil if required. Add the tamarind or lemon juice, pumpkin, coconut milk, and stock and simmer for 10 minutes or until the pumpkin is tender.

4

Heat the remaining oil in a second skillet, add the remaining shallots and sauté until crisp. Spread out on paper towels to drain. Sprinkle well with salt.

5

Divide the pumpkin between 4 bowls and serve topped with sautéed shallots, cilantro, and beansprouts.

Eight-treasure chinese squash

Dropping in to my local Chinese food shop for a bundle of bok choy, I can't help but leave with an extra bag, full of exotic dried ingredients. This recipe will, for some of us, charter unknown territory, but don't let that put you off. The shopping is easy (everything can be bought from a Chinese food shop) it's easy to make, and delicious. It's Chinese treasures packed into a squash.

6 dried shiitake mushrooms

8 dried oriental black fungus (optional)

1 tablespoon dried shrimp (optional)

1¼ cups glutinous rice, soaked overnight in a bowl of water

2 dried Chinese sausages

1 lb. cooked Chinese crispy duck and/or pork, sliced and boned

1 tablespoon light soy sauce

sesame oil

6 large pattypan-type or medium-sized round squashes*

1 teaspoon five-spice powder

salt

To serve:

chile oil

soy sauce

Serves 6

Note and variation:

This recipe is also illustrated on page 2, using Little Gem squash, peeled then stuffed as in the main recipe. They were then gently poached for 25 minutes in a covered saucepan with 4 cups chicken stock, 3 tablespoons rice wine, 2 inches sliced fresh ginger, and 4 halved scallions. They were served in a pool of poaching juices.

1

Put the mushrooms, fungus, and shrimp, if using, in a bowl with cold water to cover. Soak for 30 minutes or until rehydrated. Drain.

2

Line a Chinese steamer with cheesecloth. Drain the rice and spread it over the cheesecloth, put the Chinese sausages on top, and steam over boiling water for 25 minutes, adding more boiling water to the steamer if necessary. (The rice will be sticky.)

3

Slice the sausage and mix with the rice, mushrooms, duck and/or pork, and shrimp, if using. Season with soy sauce and sesame oil.

4

Cut the tops off the squashes, remove the core and seeds, and rub the flesh with five-spice powder and salt. Stuff the rice mixture into the squashes, replace the cap, put into the steamer, and steam for about 40 minutes or until the squashes are cooked (test with the point of a knife).

5

Serve with chile oil and soy sauce.

Char-grilled chicken
and pumpkin couscous with honey, mint, and cardamom lemon oil

Don't be put off by the long list of ingredients—though there are many different spices, they are all quite ordinary things by today's standards and you probably have them in your pantry already.

⅔ cup olive oil

20 cardamom pods, crushed

1 large whole lemon, coarsely chopped

4 chicken breast fillets

1 butternut squash, halved, seeded, and thickly sliced

1½ chicken stock cubes

11 oz. couscous

torn leaves from 1 bunch of mint, plus extra to serve

a bunch of chives, finely chopped

2 red onions, halved and finely sliced

2 garlic cloves, crushed

1 teaspoon ground cumin

1 teaspoon ground coriander

½ teaspoon ground cinnamon

a pinch of saffron (optional)

2 teaspoons honey

1 tablespoon pine nuts

sea salt and freshly ground black pepper

Serves 4

1

Put the oil, cardamom pods, and lemon in a small skillet and heat gently (do not sauté) until the lemon peel is lightly stewed and softened. Let cool.

2

Season the chicken and squash and rub with some of the cardamom lemon oil. Preheat a stove-top grill pan (ridged, if you want black lines) or charcoal grill, add the chicken and squash, and cook for about 2–3 minutes on each side.

3

Dissolve the stock cubes in 4 cups boiling water. Put the couscous in a bowl and pour over enough stock to just cover (don't be tempted to add more stock). Season and let swell. Fluff through with a fork after 5 minutes. Stir in the mint and chives.

4

Heat 1 tablespoon of the oil in a large shallow saucepan, add the onions, garlic, and ground spices and sauté until the onions are soft. Add the saffron, if using, honey, pine nuts, and remaining stock. Season lightly. Add the pumpkin, put the chicken on top, and heat to simmering. Partly cover the pan with a lid, then cook for 10 minutes until the squash is just soft.

4

Divide the couscous between 4 bowls, add the spiced onion, chicken (sliced if you wish), and squash, pour over the hot juices, then serve topped with a few extra mint leaves.

Variations:

- Instead of chicken use roast duck confit (page 54).
- Use cardamom lemon oil to brush meat or vegetables before broiling or roasting.

21

Lamb shanks

with fall squash ratatouille

Lamb shank is the upper foreleg of the animal. Allow for 3 hours of slow braising—this one can't be rushed. In fact, the shanks taste better if cooked the day before (until stage 3) and left to saturate and cool in their juices; the meat will be meltingly tender and will fall from the bone.

4 lamb shanks, trimmed

3 garlic cloves, cut into slivers

2 tablespoons olive oil, for cooking, plus extra for brushing

1 large onion, finely chopped

1 large carrot, finely chopped

2 sticks celery, finely chopped

2 tablespoons tomato paste

3 bay leaves

2 strips orange peel

¾ cup white wine

2 red peppers, seeded and sliced, or 2 Italian sun-dried red peppers*

1 small butternut or acorn squash, halved lengthwise, peeled, seeded, and sliced

1 tablespoon capers

1¼ cups black olives, pitted if preferred

small bunch basil, leaves only

sea salt and freshly ground black pepper

Serves 4

From Italian gourmet stores.

1

Season the lamb shanks and stab them all over with a knife. Insert the garlic slivers into the incisions. Heat 1 tablespoon of the oil in a large, heavy-bottom skillet. Brush each shank with olive oil, add to the pan in batches, and sauté until brown on all sides. Remove and set aside. Add the remaining oil to the skillet and heat gently.

2

Add the onion, carrot, and celery and sauté until browned. Mix in the tomato paste, bay leaves, orange peel, and seasoning. Cook for 2 minutes. Add the wine and ¾ cup water, bring to a boil, then simmer until reduced by half. Transfer to a small, deep roasting pan.

3

Add the lamb shanks to the pan, cover tightly with foil and cook in a preheated oven at 300°F for about 2 hours.

4

Heat the remaining oil in the skillet. Brush the peppers with olive oil and season with salt and freshly ground black pepper. Add to the skillet and cook until lightly browned on both sides. Add to the lamb shanks, then add the squash, capers, olives, and a little extra water if necessary. Continue braising for 1 hour or until the squash is tender.

5

Remove from the oven, then top with the basil leaves and serve with creamy mashed potato or crusty bread.

Nuts are eaten throughout the world; before, during, and after meals; salted, toasted, dry-roasted, sautéed, spiced, or plain; or simply cracked from the shell. They are a world staple and are used in many cooked dishes: sauces, stuffings, curries, pie shells, and pastries are thickened and packed with ground or whole nuts. Each region has its favorites: in Britain it's hazelnuts and chestnuts; in Spain, it's chiefly almonds; Italy, pine nuts; Africa, peanuts; the Middle East, almonds, pine nuts, and pistachios; India, almonds and cashews; Southeast Asia, coconuts and candlenuts; and America, pecans and peanuts.

Nuts are protein-rich, full of vitamins, calcium, iron, and oils (and calories, too, unfortunately). Because of their high oil content they should not be stored for too long or in too warm conditions—the resinous oil can turn rancid. So buy them as you need them and make a point of enjoying them in Fall when they're in season—sweet and milky. My favorites for cooking are hazelnuts and cob nuts, roasted, skinned, and baked into a crisp meringue or cake—they are the toasty scent of Fall. They are also the easiest to crack!

There's an art to cracking a nut. The conventional nutcracker, for me, is not up to it. The metal grippers splinter the edible part of the nut everywhere. I'm always left with a few meager scraps of kernel held firmly between feisty pieces of shell hanging on for dear life, and shell scraps all over the table and floor.

I can manage hazelnuts, which always seem to come out whole, but maybe everyone has their favorite nut, one that performs and behaves for them (one person's walnut heaven is another's walnut hell).

Screw-mechanism nut crackers are pretty accurate: designed for perfect crack control, a bit like a thumbscrew, they stop your nuts from flying everywhere. But let's be serious: the best way to crack nuts is not with any man-made device, but with a simple stone. Not your usual handy kitchen or table utensil, I know, but it works (for me) and I keep a rounded stone for this purpose (plus other culinary purposes too). All you need is a gentle, centralized tap and the nut usually opens precisely, with minimum splinter velocity. It's perfect.

nuts

Spice island dumplings

The spice islands of Indonesia still retain their plantations of nutmeg, cloves cinnamon, and nuts. I dreamt up this recipe while sitting on top of an island volcano, looking over the spice groves below. It contains all the flavors of Indonesia in a nut dumpling, simply prepared and cooked.

6 cups light chicken stock

2 stalks lemongrass, trimmed and smashed

8 kaffir lime leaves, torn,
or the juice of ½ lime, plus 1 teaspoon sugar

2 garlic cloves, thickly sliced

1½ inches fresh ginger, thickly sliced

1 package rice vermicelli noodles, about 1 oz., soaked in hot water for 4 minutes, drained, and rinsed

Chinese leaves, such as bok choy

Spice dumplings:

8 oz. peeled shrimp, fresh or frozen and thawed

8 oz. ground pork

1½ inches fresh ginger, peeled and finely grated

2 tablespoons finely chopped cilantro

2½ oz. canned bamboo shoots, drained

16 macadamia nuts

4 scallions, trimmed and chopped

2 small red chiles, finely chopped

½ tablespoon *kecap manis* or dark soy sauce

1 tablespoon fish sauce or 1 teaspoon salt

2 tablespoons lime juice

a pinch of ground cloves

a pinch of ground cinnamon

1 small egg, lightly beaten, to bind

vegetable oil, for sautéing

Serves 4

1

Put the chicken stock, lemongrass, lime leaves or juice and sugar, garlic, and ginger in a saucepan, bring to a boil, and simmer, covered, for about 20 minutes. Taste and add salt if necessary. Strain into a clean pan and discard the flavorings.

2

To make the dumplings, put the shrimp in a food processor and chop for 1–2 seconds. Transfer to a bowl. Add all the remaining ingredients except the egg and oil to the processor and work to a coarse crumb consistency. Mix with the shrimp and egg. Roll the mixture into walnut-sized balls and chill for 30 minutes.

3

Heat the oil in a skillet or deep-fryer, add the dumplings in batches and cook gently until golden brown all over, about 2–3 minutes. Remove and set aside.

4

To serve, reheat the broth and arrange a share of noodles and a few leaves in 4 deep soup bowls. Divide the dumplings between the bowls and pour over the hot lime broth.

Variations:
• Use Brazil nuts instead of macadamia nuts.
• Spear each dumpling with a bamboo skewer, sauté, and serve with drinks.

Persian chicken with coconut and pistachios

Coconut is one of the most delicious of all nuts—and thankfully it is available all year round. Almonds and pistachios are typical of Persian and Moghul cooking, prized for their color as well as flavor. The curry improves with time, so try to make it the day before.

4 chicken legs, skinned and cut into thigh and drumstick pieces

¼ teaspoon ground cinnamon

¼ teaspoon ground cloves

⅓ cup sunflower oil

6 garlic cloves, chopped

1½ inches fresh ginger, chopped

¼ cup blanched whole almonds

2 onions, chopped

4 dried chiles

6 black cardamom pods, bruised

4 teaspoons garam masala*

6 tablespoons plain yogurt

1 cup canned coconut milk

2 tablespoons golden raisins

salt

To serve:

finely grated flesh of ½ fresh coconut

1 tablespoon slivered nuts, such as almonds and pistachios

4 small bananas, sliced (optional)

Serves 4

Note: *Garam masala is sold in gourmet stores and Asian, especially Indian, markets. If unavailable, use half ground cinnamon, half chile powder. The whole chiles and cardamoms are for flavoring —tell your guests not to eat them.*

1

Put the garlic, ginger, almonds, and onions in a food processor and work to a paste, adding a drop of water if necessary.

2

Rub the chicken pieces with the cinnamon, cloves, and a little salt. Heat the oil in a non-stick skillet, add the chicken, and sauté on all sides until golden. Transfer to a flameproof casserole dish. Retain the oil in the skillet.

3

Add the chiles and black cardamom pods to the oil and sauté until the chiles blister. Add the onion mixture and garam masala and sauté until the paste darkens—keep stirring to avoid burning. Strain off excess oil.

4

Slowly stir in the yogurt, 1 tablespoon at a time, then stir in the coconut milk, ½ cup water, and the raisins. Pour around the chicken in the casserole dish and heat to simmering. Cook, covered, in a preheated oven at 300°F for 1 hour.

5

Serve topped with grated coconut, slivered nuts, and banana, if using.

Beef stew with chestnuts

You have to have patience to prepare and peel fresh chestnuts—it's a real fiddle. However you can now buy stress-free, vacuum-packed chestnuts, which have been peeled and part-cooked—they taste delicious and take all the hard work out of chestnut preparation.

3 lb. blade or
stewing beef,
cut into 4 pieces*

3½ tablespoons
beef dripping or
olive oil

1 large onion,
finely chopped

2 garlic cloves,
crushed

2 bay leaves

1 star anise
(optional)

2 carrots,
finely chopped

2 celery stalks,
finely chopped

1 tablespoon
tomato purée

1½ bottles red wine

18 chestnuts

1 teaspoon sugar

salt and freshly
ground black
pepper

Serves 6–8

1

Rub the meat with salt and plenty of pepper. Heat a heavy, flameproof casserole dish until hot, add 2 tablespoons dripping or oil, and add the meat. Leave without moving until well browned and caramelized, about 2 minutes. Turn over and continue browning until all sides are done. Remove from the casserole dish.

2

Add 1 tablespoon dripping or oil, add the onion, garlic, bay leaves, star anise, if using, carrots, and celery and sauté until browned. Add salt and pepper, stir in the tomato purée, and cook for 1 minute. Add the wine and 1¼ cups water, bring to a boil, then simmer until reduced by half.

3

Put the meat back into the casserole dish with the vegetable-wine mixture, cover, and let braise gently in a preheated oven at 300°F for 3 hours.

4

If using fresh chestnuts, part-slice the chestnut skins open on their curved side, then boil for 5 minutes. Strain, cool, then peel and remove the brown pith. Cut in half. Heat the remaining dripping or oil in a skillet, add the sugar and chestnuts, and sauté until caramelized, about 3 minutes. Add to the casserole dish, then return to the oven to braise for a further 40 minutes. Serve with buttery mashed potato flavored with mustard or horseradish.

*** Note:** Try to use blade of beef (from the shoulder) for this recipe: it is marbled with fat and connective tissue and especially suited to long, slow cooking. The meat is lubricated as it cooks, becoming moist and tender.*

Pecan pork with apple and maple syrup

Pecans taste like walnuts, but a touch sweeter. You'll need string and bamboo skewers to tie the pork. Remove the string before serving, but leave the skewers in the meat to hold each piece together.

1 loin of pork (about 3 lb.), trimmed but with skin included

½ teaspoon ground allspice

3 tablespoons olive oil

5 tablespoons maple syrup

2 tablespoons butter

6 apples, cored and quartered

salt and freshly ground black pepper

Pecan stuffing:

1½ cups shelled pecans

1 onion, chopped

2 garlic cloves, crushed

leaves from 1 bunch of flat-leaf parsley

1 bunch of sage, stems discarded

2 cups fresh breadcrumbs

2 cloves, ground

1 egg, lightly beaten

salt and freshly ground black pepper

Serves 4

1

To make the stuffing, work the nuts in a food processor until finely chopped but not ground. Transfer to a large bowl. Add the onion, garlic, and herbs to the processor and chop finely.

2

Heat 2 tablespoons olive oil in a skillet, add the onion mixture, and cook gently until softened. Stir into the pecan mixture, then stir in the ground cloves, salt, pepper, and egg. Open up the natural cavity in the meat and stuff with the pecan stuffing. Close up and tie the length of the loin with string.

3

Place the meat in a roasting pan. Using a craft knife or very sharp kitchen knife, score the skin and fat crosswise with fine parallel slashes. After scoring, place the fat on top of the roast, then secure at regular intervals with skewers. Rub with plenty of salt, pepper, allspice, and the remaining oil. Roast in a preheated oven at 425°F for about 30 minutes. Pour over half the maple syrup, lower the heat to 375°F, then roast for a further 45 minutes.

4

Heat the butter in a skillet, add the apple quarters, and sauté until lightly browned. Pour in the remaining maple syrup and cook for about 2 minutes until lightly caramelized. Arrange around the pork for the last 10 minutes of cooking. Remove from the oven and set aside, loosely covered with foil, for 10 minutes before carving. To serve, slice the pork as skewered pieces and serve with mashed celeriac or parsnip.

Caramel nut shortbread

Caramel squares, often found in old-fashioned bakeries, cafés, and English tea shops, are deliciously decadent. Sweetly addictive, they will work wonders (in the wrong direction) to your waistline. Eat one, do 80 push-ups, that's the way to do it. I make mine with nuts and raisins.

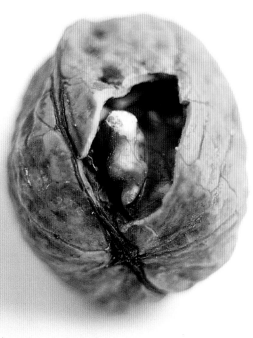

2 cups all-purpose flour

a pinch of salt

½ cup plus 2 tablespoons sugar

1 cup unsalted butter

1¼ cups plump raisins

2¼ cups pecan or walnut halves

7 oz. bitter chocolate

Caramel:

½ cup unsalted butter

½ cup plus 2 tablespoons raw sugar

2 tablespoons light corn syrup

6 oz. sweetened condensed milk (1 small can)

Serves 4

12- x 8-inch jelly roll pan

1

To make the shortbread, put the flour, salt, sugar, and butter into a food processor and pulse until the dough forms a ball. Alternatively, using your fingertips, rub the butter into the flour until the mixture resembles fine crumbs, then work in the salt and sugar. Press the mixture into the jelly roll pan and smooth with the back of a knife. Sprinkle with raisins and press flat. Bake in a preheated oven at 350°F for 20–25 minutes.

2

Put all the caramel ingredients in a non-stick saucepan and heat gently, but do not boil. Beat thoroughly together.

3

Line the nuts across the cooked shortbread base, then pour over the hot caramel mixture. Smooth with a spatula and chill until firm.

4

Melt the chocolate in a heatproof bowl set over a saucepan of gently simmering water. Pour the chocolate over the set caramel mixture, smooth with a spatula, and let set. Cut into slices or fingers before serving.

Hazelnut tiramisu cake

The flavor of hazelnuts is heightened when they're roasted. Roast the shelled nuts for ten minutes in a moderate oven and rub off the papery skins with a kitchen towel.

4 eggs

1¼ cups sugar

1¼ cups all-purpose flour, sieved

⅔ cup hazelnuts, roasted, skinned, and coarsely ground

1 teaspoon vanilla extract

Tiramisu filling:

2 eggs

2 tablespoons sugar

1½ lb. mascarpone

1 cup heavy cream

½ cup strong coffee (cold)

¼ cup coffee liqueur, such as Kahlua

unsweetened cocoa powder, for dusting (optional)

Chocolate band (optional):*

11 oz. bitter chocolate, broken into pieces

Serves 4

2 round 7-inch springform cake pans, buttered and base-lined with greaseproof paper

1

To make the cake, beat the eggs with an electric beater or mixer until frothy. Gradually beat in the sugar until the mixture is absolutely white and holds its shape. Fold in the flour, hazelnuts, and vanilla. Divide the mixture between the 2 buttered cake pans. Bake in a preheated oven at 350°F for 25–30 minutes, or until firm to the touch. Let cool, then remove the paper and slice each sponge into 2 rounds.

2

To make the filling, beat the eggs with the sugar in a large bowl, then beat in the mascarpone. Reserve one-third of the mixture in a small bowl. Beat the cream to soft peak stage and fold into the mixture in the large bowl. Mix the coffee with the coffee liqueur in a cup or pitcher.

3

To assemble the cake, put a round of sponge on a serving plate and sprinkle with the liqueur coffee mixture. Cover with a thick layer of mascarpone cream. Top with another round of sponge and repeat the process until all the sponge has been used. (Don't sprinkle coffee right to the edges and leave the top sponge unsprinkled.) Using a spatula, cover the top and the sides of the cake with a layer of the reserved mascarpone. Chill until serving and dust with cocoa powder if you like.

__Note:__ To make the Chocolate Band casing, put the chocolate into a heatproof bowl set over a saucepan of simmering water. Melt until smooth and lump-free. Cut out a rectangle of card measuring the outside circumference of the cake pan x height of the cake. Set on a large, smooth work surface. Pour the chocolate over the card, spreading with a spatula until the edges are covered. Smooth level. Let cool a little but not set. When the chocolate loses its "gloss", carefully excavate along one short edge of the card, lift up, and peel away from the work surface. Bend the chocolate-covered card around the cake (chocolate on the inside) with a small overlapping "seam" and secure with tape. Refrigerate until set, then remove the tape and carefully peel off the card.

"Mushrooms on toast"—it says it all. It would be my last meal on Earth. It's pure mushroominess, it's Fall, it's the one meal I can never tire of, and the simplest mushroom dish of all. But I'm not talking any old mushroom on toast: it has to be either the giant flat-cap field mushrooms or a host of perfect pearly little buttons, preferably so fresh and dewy as if plucked that morning. Unfortunately it's the cultivated variety that reaches my plate. Forest mushrooms are hard to come by in my part of the world.

The good thing about mushrooms is you have to do so little to them before cooking. All they need is a gentle brushing to remove any dirt (never wash them), trim off any woody stems, then sauté quickly in butter or olive oil with seasoning, chopped garlic and chopped parsley.

Mix them with salad, pasta, rice, or potatoes, or you could embellish them with a softly poached egg—the possibilities positively mushroom.

Depending on where you live, there can be dozens of cultivated "wild" funghi to choose from. The most common include delicate oyster mushrooms, smoky, meaty shiitakes, weird enokii, and the king of mushrooms, the heady porcini or cepes. Other "wild" mushrooms are often sold fresh in Fall—buy them and try them. Please be warned, some mushrooms are poisonous and can be deadly. This book is not designed to, and does not, provide you with the information necessary to pick or identify species of "wild" mushrooms. It is extremely important that you only purchase mushrooms from a merchant that you can trust; if you have any reason to doubt the identification of your mushrooms, do not cook or eat them.

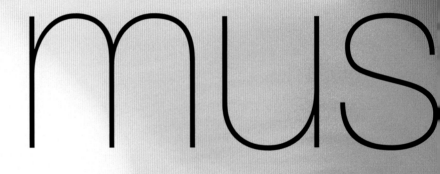

hrooms

Roasted mushrooms

with horseradish mascarpone

Mushrooms on toast are, for me, the definitive mushroom meal. Simple and straight to the point. Though I don't usually like to mess around with it, this recipe with hot horseradish and thyme still follows the purist path—the combination is wonderful.

6 large open mushrooms, stems removed, caps well brushed

a bunch of thyme

½ cup butter, softened, plus extra, for greasing

3 garlic cloves, crushed

6 thick slices white bread, toasted

sea salt and freshly ground black pepper

Horseradish mascarpone:

2 inches fresh horseradish root, peeled and grated, or 2 tablespoons horseradish sauce

1 cup mascarpone cheese

Serves 6

1

Thoroughly mix the horseradish and mascarpone and set aside.

2

Put the mushrooms, gills upward, in a greased roasting pan. Sprinkle with sea salt and pepper and tuck the thyme around them.

3

Mix two-thirds of the butter with the garlic and dot over the mushrooms. Roast in a preheated oven at 375°F for about 10 minutes.

4

Spread the toast with the remaining butter. Add a mushroom and a spoonful of horseradish mascarpone to each slice. Sprinkle with the thyme leaves and serve.

Porcini pizza with garlic butter

Porcini—"little pigs" in Italian—are also known as cepes and are the kings of the mushroom family. Their flavor is rich and intense—the very essence of mushroominess. Don't make this with dried porcini, which should only be used in sauces, stocks, and braises. Use other "wild" mushrooms instead.

½ cup butter

14 oz. fresh porcini, sliced, or other mushrooms, wiped clean and woody stem ends removed

3 garlic cloves, crushed

2 mozzarella, thinly sliced

3 sprigs of rosemary

salt and freshly ground black pepper

Pizza dough:

½ oz. fresh yeast

3⅓ cups Italian *tipo 00* flour or all-purpose flour

1 teaspoon salt

a pinch of sugar

fine semolina, for dusting

Makes 4 or 12 pizzette

1

To make the pizza dough, dissolve the yeast in 1 cup warm water. Pile the flour on a work surface and make a well in the center. Add the yeast mixture, salt, and sugar. Mix to a soft dough, then knead until silky and elastic. Dust with flour, put in a bowl, cover, and leave in a warm place for about 1 hour until doubled in size.

2

To make the topping, heat the butter in a wide skillet, add the sliced porcini, and sauté briefly on both sides. Stir in the garlic and seasoning and remove from the heat. Heat a lightly oiled, heavy baking tray in the oven, set at its highest setting, until very hot.

3

Punch down the risen dough with your knuckles and divide into 4 or 12 pieces. Flatten each with a rolling pin and, using your fingers (or rolling pin), stretch into long, flat, oval shapes. Dust on both sides with semolina. Brush with the garlic butter, sprinkle with slices of mozzarella, and top with the porcini and the leaves from the sprigs of rosemary. Arrange on the preheated baking tray and bake at the same temperature for 10–15 minutes for large or 8 minutes for small.

Mushroom salad with homemade chips

This is the quintessential warm mushroom salad that can be quickly put together in a matter of minutes. Homemade potato chips make the salad special and they aren't difficult to make (though of course if you insist, you can use a bag of crinkle-cut store-bought chips instead).

1 lb. mixed mushrooms

2 garlic cloves

leaves from 1 small bunch of flat-leaf parsley, coarsely chopped

autumn salad leaves, such as baby red chard, baby spinach leaves, and oak leaf lettuce

balsamic vinegar, to taste

salt and freshly ground black pepper

virgin olive oil, for frying and dressing

Homemade chips:

3 large baking potatoes

oil, for frying

1

Using a mandoline slicer or food processor fitted with a slicing attachment, finely slice the potatoes. To achieve the cross-hatched line effect, use the serrated blade on the mandoline, set to fine slice, turning the potato 90 degrees after each slice. Soak the slices in cold water for 30 minutes.

2

Drain the potato slices and pat dry. Fill a wok one-third full of oil, or a deep-fryer to the recommended level. Heat the oil to 375°F, add the potatoes, and fry in batches until crisp and golden. Drain on crumpled paper towels.

3

Put the salad leaves in a bowl. Heat 4 tablespoons olive oil in a skillet, add the mushrooms, garlic, salt, and pepper, and sauté gently until the mushrooms are nicely browned. Stir in the parsley, then immediately tip the mushrooms and their oil over the leaves. Toss, season, and sprinkle with balsamic vinegar. Serve with the chips.

Serves 4

Mushroom and truffled potato lasagne

The lasagne can be prepared and cooked a few hours ahead—simply reheat for 20 minutes before serving. In fact it holds its shape and cuts better if it has been precooked. Truffle-infused oil is vital for the success of this recipe. If you can't find fresh porcini make sure you add a few slices of dried porcini instead, but soak them first. I used a deep pan to make mine—it's fine to use your regular favorite lasagne dish instead, but remember to double up on the ingredients if yours is very large.

2 lb. baking potatoes

½ cup light cream

¼ cup butter, plus extra for greasing

1 tablespoon truffle oil, plus extra for serving

2 tablespoons olive oil, for sautéing

8 oz. mixed "wild" or large cap mushrooms, sliced (include some porcini, fresh or dried)

10 lasagne pasta sheets, cooked according to package instructions (don't use the bake-only variety)

4 oz. Taleggio cheese, or other soft cheese, thinly sliced

1 tablespoon milk, for brushing

sea salt and freshly ground black pepper

Serves 4–6

1

Cook the potatoes in salted water until soft, then mash with the cream, butter, and truffle oil—this will produce a softer mash than normal. Taste and adjust the seasoning.

2

Heat the olive oil in a skillet, add the mushrooms, and sauté for about 3 minutes until just cooked and tinged brown at the edges. Season with salt and freshly ground black pepper.

3

Butter a deep pan or baking dish, approximately 7 x 5 inches. Place a layer of the cooked lasagne sheets over the bottom of the dish, cover with a layer of mushrooms, spread with a thick layer of mashed potato, and cover this with thinly sliced cheese.

4

Repeat this process about 3 times or until you have used up all the potato mixture and have enough pasta and mushrooms left for one final layer. Arrange the remaining mushrooms across the top layer of pasta, moisten with milk, cover with foil, and bake in a preheated oven at 350°F for 40 minutes.

Variations:

• If you're feeling very rich, instead of mushrooms, shave paper-thin slices of white truffle over the top before serving, as in the photograph. At over $1200 a pound, this is obviously not an everyday practice!

Chicken and mushroom pie

Though Spring is the season for morels, with their distinctive smoky flavor they are such an important culinary mushroom that I had to include them here. Dried morels are available all year round and, picked and dried in their prime, can be much better than many "fresh" ones.

1 lb. fresh ready-made shortcrust pastry dough

6 tablespoons butter, softened

1 whole cooked chicken, about 3 lb.

1 onion, quartered

2 garlic cloves

1 fresh bouquet garni of bay leaves, parsley, and leek

3 blades mace or a pinch of powdered mace

2 cups good chicken stock

12 fresh morels, brushed clean, or 40 g dried (soaked in water until soft) or a mixture of "wild" mushrooms, including morels

1 tablespoon all-purpose flour

¼ cup heavy cream

1 egg, lightly beaten

salt and freshly ground black pepper

1 fresh chanterelle, to serve (optional)

Serves 4

1
Roll out the pastry dough to ⅛ inch thick. Spread two-thirds of the butter over half the dough and fold the other half over the top. Repeat and fold twice more. Press together and chill for 30 minutes (this will make the pastry flaky).

2
Flake the chicken into chunks. Discard the skin and bones.

3
Put the onion, garlic, bouquet garni, mace, and stock in a saucepan, bring to a boil, then simmer for 10 minutes. Boil until reduced by three-quarters. Strain and discard the solids.

4
Heat the remaining butter in a skillet, add the morels, and sauté for 1–2 minutes. Add the flour and cook to a paste. Stir in the reduced stock and simmer to form a thick sauce. Add the cream and cooked mushrooms and let boil for about 2 minutes. Taste and adjust the seasoning.

5
Roll out half the dough and use to line a 7-inch greased pie dish. Roll out the remaining dough and slice into ribbons about 2 inches wide. Weave together. Fill the pie shell with the chicken and mushrooms. Pour in the cream sauce. Brush the top edge of the pie shell with beaten egg and arrange the dough weave on top. Trim the edges and then press together. Brush with beaten egg and bake in a preheated oven at 350°F for 1 hour. Serve, topped with the fresh chanterelle, if using.

Pork chops with peppered mushroom gravy

No-nonsense pork chops with a rich autumnal mushroom gravy and a bowl of mashed potato to mop it up—soul-warming stuff. Any mixture of "wild" funghi will do, including chanterelles and porcini, but you can also achieve good results with large open-cap mushrooms or smaller ones, just larger than buttons (slip in few slices of dried porcini to get the "wild" flavor).

3 tablespoons butter

2 tablespoons olive oil

3 garlic cloves, finely chopped

1 large onion, chopped

3 bay leaves

3 tablespoons sherry vinegar

¾ cup sherry or Madeira

1 oz. dried porcini, soaked in ⅔ cup hot water until soft

3 cups chicken stock

4 pork chops, trimmed of excess fat

12 oz. mixed "wild" and cultivated mushrooms

sea salt and freshly ground black pepper

creamy mashed potato, to serve (optional)

Serves 4

1

Heat half the butter and half the olive oil in a skillet, add half the garlic, the onion, bay leaves, and seasoning, and sauté until the onion becomes translucent. Add the sherry vinegar and reduce until almost dry, then add the sherry, the porcini, their soaking water, and the stock to the skillet and simmer for 20 minutes or until reduced by half. Strain into a clean, wide saucepan and discard all the residue, including the porcini.

2

Heat a ridged stove-top grill pan or heavy-bottom skillet until smoking hot. Rub the pork with salt, pepper, and a little of the olive oil and char-grill for 4 minutes on each side.

3

Cut medium-sized mushrooms in half, trim off any woody stem tips, and slice any large-cap mushrooms. Heat the remaining oil and butter in the skillet, add the mushrooms and the remaining garlic, and sauté about 2 minutes or until tinged golden brown. Season, then add to the pan of gravy and reheat.

4

Serve the chops, mushroom gravy, and mashed potato, if using, on preheated plates and sprinkle generously with pepper.

Apples are an easy fruit. Easy because they're easy to eat—there's no peeling (unless you're one of those fussy peel-all-fruit people) and, once they're picked, there's no waiting for them to ripen. They're easy on the tongue—crisp and refreshing, and easy on the eye—the most instant of instant packaged meals. Sliced, sautéed, puréed, and baked, they're a versatile and goodly lot.

I'm not a fan of whole baked apples—stuff them with whatever you like, there's no getting away from that blistering "school dessert" effect: a scorched mouth and a mush of endless, rather bland apple. Apples need sugar—whole baked ones never seem to get the sweetness baked into them. Those I do love are small and full of flavor, and baked in caramel, as in tarte Tatin. (Yes please!) Or chopped up and baked into a pie with blackberries and lots of crumble on top. Or proper French glazed apple pies—wafer-thin, tart yet sweet.

Apples have an affinity with butter, cream, and alcohol—the apple-based Calvados and cider being obvious natural partners—while sugar sprinkled on top strengthens the apple's shape-holding properties. Apples don't, however, go well with other fruits, other than blackberries and dried fruits, but are wonderful with pork, game birds, and cheese—especially salty and cream cheeses.

Granny Smith apples (a chance hybrid discovered last century by an Australian —yes, she was a grandmother, and her name was Smith) hold their shape well when cooking and are excellent for open tarts, as are Golden Delicious. I like Greening apples or Northern Spy apples for pie fillings and purées—their flavor seems to intensify under heat.

Some heirloom varieties, of which there are several thousand, are now being reintroduced to our markets. They are aromatic and well worth trying, making a welcome change from the "over-bred" disease-resistant supermarket varieties. Crab apples, the ancestor of our cultivated apple, are too sour to eat fresh, but make wonderful jelly for serving with pork or sausages.

In fact—apples are the perfect food. All you need is a wedge of mature cheese and one bottle of wine—and lunch is fixed. Simple.

apples

Apple duck confit

with spiced baked beans

Duck confit is easy to make, but does require forethought. Make it in quantity, say 10 pieces at a time—it will keep for at least a year in the fridge and you'll have it on hand for when you want an instant impressive dinner. It's as fast as a ready-made meal but miles ahead in flavor. If you don't want to make it yourself, buy canned duck confit from a good gourmet store, or use roast duck with the spiced beans instead—it's delicious too.

4 pieces duck confit, store-bought or homemade

1 onion, chopped

3 garlic cloves, crushed

1½ inches fresh ginger

3 tablespoons vegetable oil, for sautéing

¼ teaspoon ground turmeric

3 teaspoons garam masala*, freshly ground if possible

1 large baking apple, peeled, cored, and chopped

4 small whole red chiles

1 tablespoon sweet mango chutney

3 tomatoes, peeled and finely chopped

1 tablespoon golden raisins

⅔ cup good chicken stock

2 cups canned cannellini beans or lima beans, drained and rinsed

salt and black pepper

Serves 4

* Available from Asian stores. If difficult to find, use half ground cinnamon and half chile powder.

1

Roast the duck pieces in a preheated oven at 400°F for about 15–20 minutes or until golden.

2

Put the onion, garlic, and ginger in a food processor and blend to a paste.

3

Heat the oil in a skillet, add the onion mixture, the turmeric, and 2 teaspoons of the garam masala and sauté until browned. Season, add the chopped apple, chiles, mango chutney, tomatoes, sultanas, chicken stock, and drained beans and simmer until reduced and thickened, about 10–15 minutes.

4

Sprinkle with the remaining garam masala and divide between 4 heated bowls. Add 1 duck leg to each bowl and serve.

Note: To prepare duck confit at home, trim the excess fat from 4 duck legs and arrange them in a shallow dish, skin side up. Sprinkle with 3 tablespoons salt, 3 sliced garlic cloves, and crumble over a few dried bay leaves. Turn to coat, cover, and chill for 2 days, turning once. Rinse the legs under cold water to remove the salt, then pat dry. Heat 2 lb. lard or duck fat in a deep saucepan, add the duck legs, and simmer very gently without frying for 1½ hours. Ladle a little of the fat into a deep, narrow container and, using tongs, place the cooked legs on top. Pour in the remaining fat until completely covered (do not include any of the meat juices at the bottom of the pan). Store in the refrigerator until needed.

Pot-roasted game bird

with apple, cabbage, juniper, and cream

A cross between a roast and a stew, you can put this dish in the oven, set the timer, and forget about it. This method keeps the bird moist and tender so the meat will fall from the bones, just the way you want it.

1 game bird, such as pheasant
or guinea fowl, or a chicken, well seasoned

3 tablespoons olive oil

¼ cup butter

8 small pickling onions or shallots

2 garlic cloves, crushed

8 juniper berries, crushed

¾ cup hard cider

⅔ cup good chicken stock

8 baby apples or 4 large, cored and quartered

greens such as the outer leaves of a
Savoy cabbage, red brussels tops, or
other cabbage, separated into leaves,
thick ribs removed

⅔ cup heavy cream

salt and freshly ground black pepper

Serves 4

1

Heat the oil and half the butter in a large skillet, add the bird, and brown it on all sides. Transfer to a deep, snug-fitting, flameproof casserole dish.

2

Wipe the skillet, then add the remaining butter, onions, garlic, and juniper and sauté gently for 2 minutes. Pour in the cider and stock. Simmer for 5 minutes. Add the apples and transfer to the casserole dish.

3

Heat to simmering, cover with a lid, then transfer to a preheated oven and cook at 350°F for 45 minutes.

4

Blanch the cabbage leaves in boiling water for 3 minutes, then tuck the leaves around the bird, pour over the cream, return to the oven, and cook for a further 15 minutes.

5

Cut the bird into pieces and serve with the apple, cabbage, and juices. Other good accompaniments are sautéed potatoes or potatoes mashed with parsnips, then flavored with truffle oil.

Apple griddlecakes with blackberries

I first cooked this outdoors in a heavy skillet over a wood fire with blackberries picked from the hedge—apple and berries are a delicious combination.

2–3 baskets blackberries

½ cup sugar

2 baking apples, peeled, cored, and diced

⅔ cup wholemeal flour

⅔ cup self-rising flour

1 teaspoon baking powder

½ teaspoon mixed spice

½ cup butter, softened, plus extra for frying

1 egg, beaten

1 tablespoon buttermilk

whipped cream or crème fraîche, to serve

Makes 2 large or 8 small

1

Put ½ basket blackberries in a saucepan with 1 tablespoon sugar. Add 1 tablespoon water and heat until the fruit breaks down —about 10 minutes. Set aside.

2

Put the diced apple into a saucepan and cook until softened but still in chunks.

3

Mix the flours, baking powder, remaining sugar, and spice in a bowl. Rub in the butter to make coarse crumbs. Mix in the apple, egg, and buttermilk to make a wet dough.

4

Heat a heavy ovenproof skillet, then brush with butter. Drop large spoonfuls of the mixture onto the skillet and lightly flatten with your hand. If you wish to make perfect circles, place a cookie cutter or tart ring in the skillet first and press the mixture to fit the ring. Reduce the heat to low and cook for 10 minutes on each side for large cakes and 4 minutes for small. Transfer to a preheated oven and bake at 350°F for about 5 minutes.

5

Put the griddlecakes on 4 small plates, cover with berries and juice, and serve with whipped cream or crème fraîche.

Baby apple pies

Pure unadulterated apple. No fancy flavors or hidden extras—apples can make it on their own. Cooked until silky smooth with a few little chunks for texture, then baked inside a buttery crumbly pastry, this is real comfort food.

2½ cups all-purpose flour

1 cup sugar, plus extra for dusting

¾ cup butter, softened

3 egg yolks

mascarpone cheese, to serve

Apple filling:

4 large baking apples,
peeled, cored, and chopped

¼ cup sugar

juice of ½ lemon

Makes about 12

one 12-hole muffin tray

1

Put the flour in a large bowl, make a well in the center, and add the sugar. Add the butter and egg yolks. Using a fork, mash the yolks, butter, and sugar together, then draw in the flour. Using your hands, mix well, then transfer to a work surface and knead well for about 30 seconds to form a smooth dough (add a little extra flour if necessary, to form the right consistency). Wrap in plastic and chill for 20 minutes.

2

Put the chopped apple in a saucepan with the sugar, lemon juice, and 2 tablespoons water and cook to a coarse purée, leaving a few lumps. Taste and add more sugar if you prefer. Cool, then chill.

3

Roll out the dough to ⅛ inch thick. Using a cookie cutter, stamp out 12 circles big enough to line the holes in a 12-hole muffin tray. Cut 12 smaller circles for lids. Line the molds with the dough and fill with the apple mixture. Brush the rim of the dough with water, top with the smaller circles of dough, and gently press the edges together. Trim with a knife to make neat edges. Make 3 small neat holes in the top of each pie and dust with sugar.

4

Bake in a preheated oven at 375°F for 20–25 minutes until golden at the edges. Cool a little, then remove, dust with more sugar, and serve with mascarpone.

61

Caramel syrup apples

with thick whipped cream

I love tarte Tatin—the soaked flaky pastry is good, but what makes it for me is the combination of melting apple saturated in caramel and all that extra buttery syrup that runs in rivulets into a pool of cream on the plate. So why not do just that. Forget about pastry, and have apples, buttery caramel, and loads of cream. A seriously sensuous windfall in a bowl.

8 small apples

juice of 1 lemon

2½ cups sugar

½ cup butter

1 teaspoon ground cinnamon

1 cup heavy cream, whipped, or crème fraîche

Serves 4

1

Peel the apples and put into a bowl of water mixed with lemon juice to stop them turning brown.

2

Put the sugar into a small saucepan with 1 tablespoon water, and cook over a gentle heat until golden and turned to a light caramel. Stir in the butter.

3

Drain the apples, pack into a deep dish, sprinkle with cinnamon, and pour over the toffee caramel. Cover loosely with foil and bake in a preheated oven at 350°F for 45 minutes or until the apples are very tender.

4

Serve in bowls with whipped cream or crème fraîche.

Sweet apple phyllo
with goat cheese, raisins, and honey syrup

Apple with cheese and a sweet syrup may sound a little odd, but if you analyse the flavors—salt, sweet, and sour—it isn't. I used Granny Smith apples because they hold their shape, but feel free to experiment.

2 Granny Smith apples, quartered, cored, and finely sliced

6 tablespoons butter, melted

1 tablespoon sugar

2 tablespoons honey

1 tablespoon Calvados (optional)

4 sheets phyllo pastry dough

7 oz. goat curd cheese or other soft cheese

2 tablespoons plump raisins

confectioner's sugar, for dusting

Makes 8

1

Toss the apples in 1 tablespoon of the melted butter and sprinkle with the sugar. Sear in a hot skillet on both sides until lightly caramelized, about 2 minutes.

2

Dissolve the honey in 3 tablespoons of hot water, add the Calvados, if using, and pour over the apples in the skillet. Simmer for about 1 minute, then decant the syrup into a serving bowl. Reserve the apples.

3

Cut each sheet of phyllo pastry dough into 4 rectangles. Brush half the sheets with melted butter and arrange the others on top, so you have 8 double layer rectangles.

4

Spread the center of each with curd cheese, arrange a line of apples on top, and dot with a few raisins. Fold the sides of the dough over the filling—they look best if they don't quite cover—and brush all over with more melted butter. Put on a buttered baking tray and cook in a preheated oven at 400°F for about 20–25 minutes or until crisp. Dust with confectioner's sugar and serve with the syrup for dipping.

Variations:

• Instead of apples, use apricots, dates, or figs, sprinkled with chopped pistachios and add rosewater to the cooled syrup.
• Use mincemeat, soak the raisins in Calvados, and add crumbled walnuts to the cheese.

65

A perfect pear standing on a perfect white plate is an image of total (affordable) elegance and refinement. From the Bosc, with its blushing skin and elegant shape, to classic pale yellow William or Bartlett and the portly Comice, each variety has its own character and shape. Their flesh is nectar-scented, buttery, and pumped full of juice. Despite their sophistication, they don't allow for sophisticated eating. They're one of those fruits you just can't eat politely—the juice always dribbles down your chin in a very undignified manner.

A pear can't be man-handled—it's a temperamental creature. Choose fruit that feels firm, pack it carefully (don't just sling it in your shopping basket) and eat it as soon as it ripens—it won't wait for you once it's peaked. If you leave it, it will turn "sleepy" and although it may look appetizing, the flesh will have turned mealy, literally overnight. They're not as long-suffering as apples.

Most pears are sold refrigerated and unripe, so if serving pears uncooked make sure you buy them a couple of days ahead and leave them out in a warm kitchen to ripen. Most large pears are cooking pears but if you're going to poach them, any variety will do—you don't need to fret too much whether you've found the right one. Peeled and gently simmered in a syrup flavored with vanilla, lemongrass, citrus, honey, wine, or spice, the cooked flesh is like a fine osmotic sponge. They will absorb even more of the poaching liquid's flavor if left to bathe overnight, and pears poached in red wine can be left for up to a week (in the fridge)—the wine will soak right through to the core.

I think pears are best kept whole, cooked or uncooked—you can never chop up a pear, rearrange it and make it look better. Somehow you've just lost it. As a result, all my recipes in this final chapter use whole or halved fruit.

You don't want to cook? Then serve the perfect pear on a perfect white plate—with shavings of pecorino or Parmesan, or a wedge of creamy blue cheese. Simplicity is the key with this fruit.

pears

Chocolate pears

You can simplify this recipe to make straightforward chocolate-coated poached pears—no coring and stuffing. Poach them and then coat the pears with chocolate as detailed below. Serve with cream or mascarpone, or be creative and pack in a box (this one used to contain Christmas tree decorations).

2 tablespoons raisins

¼ cup rum

3 strips orange peel

⅔ cup sugar

1 vanilla bean,
split lengthwise

12 baby pears,
peeled and cored*

4 oz. white marzipan

8 oz. bitter chocolate,
preferably with 70%
cocoa solids

heavy cream or
mascarpone, to serve
(optional)

Serves 4

*__Note:__ As you peel the
pears, put them in a
bowl of water with a
squeeze of lemon juice
so they don't turn
brown.*

1

Put the raisins and rum in a bowl and let soak until plump.

2

Put the orange peel, sugar, and vanilla bean in a wide shallow saucepan with 1 cup hot water. Bring to a boil and stir until the sugar dissolves. Add the pears and enough extra boiling water to cover the fruit. Simmer very gently until tender, about 10 minutes (depending on ripeness). Remove immediately from the poaching liquid and let cool on a wire rack.

3

Fill the cavity in each pear with a little marzipan and a few rum-soaked raisins.

4

Melt the chocolate in a heatproof bowl set over a saucepan of simmering water. Do not let the water touch the bowl. Let the melted chocolate cool a little, then spoon it over each pear until completely coated. Stand on a wire rack to set, then serve and eat on the same day.

Pear tart with Catalan custard

I've used a thin, *crème-anglaise*-style custard flavored with citrus peel, as the Spanish do to make *crème catalan*. If you like your custard thicker, add 2 teaspoons of cornstarch with the eggs and sugar.

1 tablespoon lemon juice

4 unripe pears

1 vanilla bean, split lengthwise

⅔ cup sugar

8 oz. fresh, ready-made puff pastry dough

1 egg, lightly beaten

confectioner's sugar, for dusting

Catalan custard:

1¼ cups milk

1¼ cups heavy cream

2 cinnamon sticks, broken

grated zest of ½ lemon

½ cup sugar

6 egg yolks

Serves 4

1

Put the milk, cream, cinnamon, and lemon in a saucepan and bring to a boil. Remove from the heat and set aside for 30 minutes.

2

Half fill a saucepan with water and add the lemon juice. Peel the pears and put them straight into the pan to stop browning. Add the vanilla bean and sugar, bring to a boil, and simmer for 25 minutes until just tender.

3

Roll out the dough, ⅛–¼ inch thick, and cut into long strips, big enough to fit 4 pear halves, side by side with about ½ inch between. Put on a greased baking tray. Arrange the halved pears across the dough and, with the tip of a knife, score a shallow cut in the dough around each pear. Brush all over with beaten egg. Bake in a preheated oven at 400°F for 20–30 minutes until puffed and golden.

4

Beat the sugar and egg yolks together in a bowl. Strain the milk mixture and beat into the egg mixture. Pour into a saucepan and heat gently, continuously stirring, until you have a thin custard that coats the back of the spoon (too much heat and the custard will curdle).

5

Dust the tart with confectioner's sugar, cut in wedges, and serve with custard.

Espresso pears with mascarpone

Dessert and coffee served together—entertaining couldn't be easier. You can also flavor the coffee and pears with cloves, cinnamon, or cardamom.

6 baby pears, peeled

2 cups fresh coffee (not instant)

3 tablespoons sugar

2 cinnamon sticks or 4 cloves (optional)

4 tablespoons coffee liqueur, such as Kahlua

mascarpone, to serve

unsweetened cocoa powder, for dusting (optional)

Serves 6

1

Put the pears, coffee, sugar, spices (if using), and liqueur in a saucepan and simmer gently until the fruit is tender, about 10 minutes (depending on ripeness). Let cool in the liqueur coffee for 2 hours or overnight.

2

Reheat and serve hot, in coffee cups, with the mascarpone. Dust with unsweetened cocoa powder, if using.

Variations:

• Add a square of chocolate to each cup, then fill with coffee and pears.
• Put the pears and coffee into cappuccino cups and serve with hot frothy cream dusted with unsweetened cocoa powder.

73

Honeyed vanilla pears with soft cheese

I used long, thin, elegant pears for this recipe, but any variety or shape will do. If you want to make them look completely smooth and devoid of any lines left by the peeler, rub them all over with a cloth after peeling.

4 large pears or 8 baby pears

1 vanilla bean, split lengthwise

¼ cup honey

3 tablespoons sugar

1 strip of orange peel

1 strip of lemon peel

juice of ½ lemon

robiola, ricotta, or other soft cheese, to serve

Serves 4

1

Put the pears in a snug-fitting saucepan with enough water to cover. Scrape the seeds from the vanilla bean into the pan and add the bean itself. Add the honey, sugar, the orange and lemon peel, and the lemon juice and bring to a boil.

2

Lower the heat, cover with a lid and gently poach for about 12 minutes for small pears, 20 minutes for larger, or until just cooked (test with a sharp knife, they should feel just firm in the center). Let cool in the syrup.

3

Remove the pears with a slotted spoon. Heat the pan of syrup to a rapid boil and reduce until the syrup has thickened enough to coat the back of a spoon. Serve each pear with a slice or spoonful of cheese and the syrup poured over.

Variations:

• Use yogurt cheese—mix 2 cups plain yogurt with 1 teaspoon salt and suspend in cheesecloth over a basin for 48 hours. The result will be a sharp-tasting cheese, excellent with the sweetness of the honey syrup. (You can also finely slice the citrus zest used in the syrup and mix this with the cheese).

Drunken pears with gorgonzola

You can't really beat a deliciously ripe nectar-scented pear with a salty piece of cheese. This is an embellished version, a good one for when the pears haven't ripened. The pears are best if left overnight—immersed in the wine juices, they become fully saturated with wine and spice.

1

Put all the ingredients except the cheese in a small saucepan, bring to a boil, then simmer for about 20–30 minutes or until the pears are soft. Let cool in the pan.

2

Remove the pears from the poaching liquid and slice in half lengthwise. Serve each person with 2 pear halves and a slice of cheese, or arrange the sliced pears and cheese on a platter, so that everyone can help themselves.

4 large pears, peeled

3 cinnamon sticks

4 whole cloves

¼ cup sugar

2 teaspoons allspice berries

2 teaspoons black peppercorns

2 bay leaves

1 bottle red wine (750 ml)

4 slices gorgonzola (serving size)

Serves 4

Variations:

• Serve halved ripe pears with broken chunks of Parmesan cheese, or on finely sliced Parma ham with a pile of Belgian endive dressed with walnut oil, freshly squeezed orange juice, and black pepper.

Ginger toffee pears with rice pudding

Rice pudding isn't just nursery food—it's rib-sticking good, as my grandfather used to say. Sometimes, a bit of plain honest home cooking is just what we need, but with these toffee pears, it's good enough for a dinner party.

6 unripe pears, peeled

1 vanilla bean, split lengthwise

⅔ cup sugar

juice of ½ lemon

Vanilla rice pudding:

1 cup short-grain rice

5 cups milk

¾ cup heavy cream

1 vanilla bean, split lengthwise

½ cup sugar

Ginger toffee:

2 inches fresh ginger, chopped

¾ cup sugar

3 tablespoons unsalted butter

Serves 4

1

To make the rice pudding, pour boiling water over the rice and soak for 3 minutes. Drain, put into a saucepan, add the milk, vanilla bean, and sugar and simmer gently for 30 minutes. Discard the bean, stir in the cream, and spoon into a gratin dish. Cook in a preheated oven at 300°F for 45 minutes.

2

To prepare the pears, put all the ingredients in a saucepan and cover with water. Simmer for 25–30 minutes or until tender. If not using immediately, let cool in the syrup. When ready to serve, remove from the syrup and heat through on top of the rice pudding.

3

To make the toffee, put the ginger, sugar, and 2 tablespoons water into a small saucepan and heat gently until the mixture becomes a good caramel color (watch it, as soon as it goes a deep red-amber color, it's close to burning). Stir in the butter, then add 5 tablespoons water and stir well. Strain to remove the pieces of ginger. Pour some of the toffee over the pears, and serve the rest in a pitcher.

index

A

acorn squash with ginger and seaweed 14
apples 52–65
  and maple syrup, pecan pork with 32
  cooking methods 52
  crab apple 52
  golden delicious 52
  granny smith 52, 64
  greening 52
  northern spy 52
apple:
  cabbage, juniper, and cream, pot-roasted game bird with 56
  caramel syrup, with thick whipped cream 62
  duck confit with spiced baked beans 54
  griddlecakes with blackberries 58
  pies, baby 60
  phyllo with goat cheese, raisins, and honey syrup, sweet 64
artichokes and sage, pumpkin fondue with 12

B

baby apple pies 60
beans, spiced baked, apple duck confit with 54
beef stew with chestnuts 30
blackberries, apple griddlecakes with 58

C

cabbage, juniper, and cream, pot-roasted game bird with apple, 56
cakes:
  apple griddle, with blackberries 58
  hazelnut tiramisu 36
caramel syrup apples with thick whipped cream 62
cardamom lemon oil, char-grilled chicken and pumpkin couscous with honey, mint, and 20
catalan custard, pear tart with 70
char-grilled chicken and pumpkin couscous with honey, mint, and cardamom lemon oil 20
cheese:
  espresso pears with mascarpone 72
  drunken pears with gorgonzola 76
  honeyed vanilla pears with soft cheese 74
  pumpkin fondue with artichokes and sage 12
  pumpkin soup with roasted pumpkin seeds and goat cheese 10
  roasted mushrooms with horseradish mascarpone 40
  sweet apple phyllo with goat cheese, raisins, and honey syrup 64
chestnuts, beef stew with 30
chicken:
  and mushroom pie 48
  char-grilled, and pumpkin couscous with honey, mint, and cardamom lemon oil 20
  persian chicken with coconut and pistachios 24
chinatown pumpkin 18
chocolate pears 68
coconut:
  curry, pumpkin 16
  and pistachios, persian chicken with 24
confit with spiced baked beans, apple duck 54
couscous, char-grilled chicken and pumpkin, with honey, mint, and cardamom lemon oil 20

chips, mushrooms, leaves, and homemade 44
curry, pumpkin coconut 16
custard, pear tart with catalan 70

D

drunken pears with gorgonzola 76
duck confit, apple, with spiced baked beans 54

E

espresso pears with mascarpone 72

F

fall squash ratatouille, lamb shanks with 22
fondue with artichokes and sage, pumpkin 12

G

game bird with apple, cabbage, juniper, and cream, pot-roasted 56
garlic butter, porcini pizza with 42
ginger:
  and seaweed, acorn squash with 14
  toffee pears with rice pudding 78
goat cheese:
  pumpkin soup with roasted pumpkin seeds and 10
  sweet apple phyllo with goat cheese, raisins, and honey syrup 64
gorgonzola, drunken pears 76
griddlecakes with blackberries, apple 58

H

hazelnut tiramisu cake 36

homemade chips, mushrooms, leaves, and 44
honey:
  mint, and cardamom lemon oil, char-grilled chicken and pumpkin couscous with 20
  syrup, sweet apple phyllo with goat cheese, raisins, and 64
honeyed vanilla pears with soft cheese 74
horseradish mascarpone, roasted mushrooms with 40

J

juniper, and cream, pot-roasted game bird with apple, cabbage, 56

L

lamb shanks with fall squash ratatouille 22
lasagne, mushroom and truffled potato 46

M

maple syrup, pecan pork with apple and 32
mascarpone:
  espresso pears with 72
  roasted mushrooms with horseradish 40
mushrooms 38–51
  button 38
  cepes 38
  chanterelle 48, 50
  chestnut 50
  enokii 38
  flat-cap field 38, 40, 46
  morel 48
  oyster 38
  porcini (see cepes) 38, 42, 46, 50
  preparing mushrooms 38
  shiitake 38
  truffles 46
  "wild" 38, 42, 46, 50
mushroom:
  and truffled potato lasagne 46
  mushrooms, leaves, and homemade chips 44
  mushrooms, roasted, with horseradish mascarpone 40
  pie, chicken and 48

N

nuts 24–37
  almonds 24
  candlenuts 24
  cashews 24
  chestnuts 30
  coconuts 24
  hazelnuts 24, 36
  peanuts 24

pecans 24, 32, 34
pine nuts 24
pistachios 24, 28
nuts:
  beef stew with chestnuts 30
  caramel nut shortbread 34
  hazelnut tiramisu cake 37
  pecan pork with apple and maple syrup 33
  persian chicken with coconut and pistachios 29
  spice island dumplings 26

P

pear tart with catalan custard 70
pears 66–79
  bartlett 66
  bosc 66, 74, 76
  comice 66
  william 66

pears:
  chocolate 66
  espresso, with mascarpone 72
  with gorgonzola, drunken 76
  with rice pudding, ginger toffee 78
  with soft cheese, honeyed vanilla 74
pecan pork with apple and maple syrup 32
persian chicken with coconut and pistachios 28
phyllo, sweet apple, with goat cheese, raisins, and honey syrup 64
pies:
  baby apple 60
  chicken and mushroom 48
pistachios, persian chicken with coconut and 28
pizza with garlic butter, porcini 42
porcini pizza with garlic butter 42
pork:
  pecan, with apple and maple syrup 32
  chops with peppered mushroom gravy 50
potato, truffled, lasagne, mushroom and 46
pot-roasted game bird with apple, juniper, and cream 56
pumpkin:
  chinatown 18
  couscous with honey, mint, and cardamom lemon oil, char-grilled chicken and pumpkin 20
  coconut curry 16
  fondue with artichokes and sage 12
  soup with roasted pumpkin seeds and goat cheese 10

R

ratatouille, lamb shanks with fall squash 22
rice pudding, ginger toffee pears with 78
roasted mushrooms with horseradish mascarpone 40

S

salad: mushrooms, leaves, and homemade chips 44
shortbread, caramel nut 34
soup, pumpkin, with roasted pumpkin seeds and goat cheese 10
spiced baked beans, apple duck confit with 54
spice island dumplings 26
squash 8–23
  acorn 8, 14, 22
  butternut 8, 20, 22
  chinese winter melon 8
  cooking methods 8
  crown prince 12
  hubbard 8
  little gem 2
  munchkins 8
  pattypan 8
  pumpkin 8, 10, 12, 16
  pumpkin seeds 10
  spaghetti squash 16
  turk's cap 8
  zucchini 8
sweet apple phyllo with goat cheese, raisins, and honey syrup 64

T

tart with catalan custard, pear 70
tiramisu cake, hazelnut 36
toffee pears with rice pudding, ginger 78

V

vanilla
  pears with soft cheese, honeyed 74
  rice pudding, ginger toffee pears with 78

W

whipped cream, caramel syrup apples with thick 62

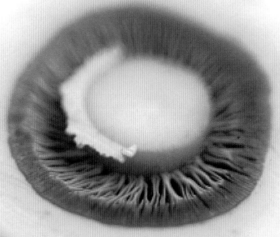

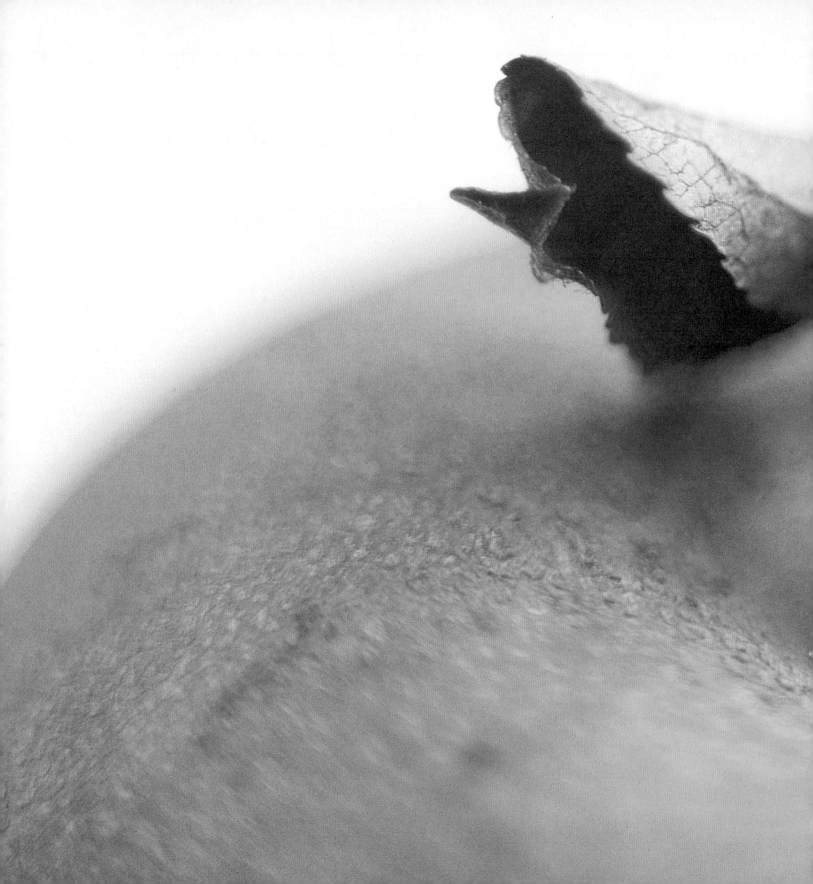